How to Become
an Event Planner

The Ultimate Guide to a Successful Career in Event Planning

by Gabriella Reznik

Table of Contents

Introduction

The event planning industry has grown massively over recent years. According to reports, individuals and groups are shelling out billions of dollars every year to organize all kinds of events. If you are looking to start a career in event planning, you will be happy to know that the market is swelling and that this type of career can be a very profitable endeavor. People will never run out of occasions to celebrate. Some people don't even need a reason to have a party. In addition, the event planning business is not limited to organizing celebrations. It also covers a variety of occasions and affairs including political rallies, conferences, business meetings, and so forth.

In general, there are three kinds of events that people celebrate regularly. There are social events, business-related events, and those that fall in between. The most common social events are outings, weddings, birthdays, graduations, and anniversaries. Business-related events will include meetings, conferences, political rallies, and product launches. Civic events, awards ceremonies, memorials, and commemorations are a mixture of social and business-related affairs.

At some point in your life, you may have had the chance to plan an event. It may have been something as small as your child's first birthday party or a wedding anniversary dinner for two. Or perhaps it might have been something as big as a Thanksgiving meal for the whole family, relatives, and friends. At work, your boss may have asked you to 'organize something' for the company Christmas Party. During these times, your event planning skills have been tested. How did it go? Was it a huge success or did you feel that some aspects of the event needed improvement? If you've discovered that the whole organization of the event made you feel exhilarated and, afterwards, fulfilled, then you might consider starting a career in event planning.

However, there are a lot of duties and responsibilities associated with being an event planner. Naturally, a person wishing to become one will need exemplary qualities to successfully accomplish all the tasks required of this job. Event planning involves the thorough preparation, organization, and management of things to make sure that everything at the event runs smoothly. Needless to say, there are various aspects of event planning that every aspiring professional party planner must know.

Interestingly, most people that have ventured into the event planning business have started with smaller aspects, such as catering, which are solely focused on one area. Others just dealt with the flowers before taking over the whole thing. An event planner will have to oversee everything including the food, venue, facilities, vendors and guests, amongst many other things. In some cases, depending on the type of occasion and the clients' needs or requests, an event planner can be in-charge of the program, rental clothes (such as for a wedding), music, transportation of clients, photography, decorations, and much more.

Why pursue a career in event planning? The answer is simple. There is a high demand for the services of an experienced event planner. Event planning requires time, expertise, and immense organizational skills which many people just don't have. However, they're willing to pay someone to organize the event for them. If you're convinced that this is the career for you, then this book will give you everything you need to know to become an event planner. You'll also find information that you can use in case you want to start your own event planning business in the future. Let's get started!

Chapter 1: Education and Certification

Often the very first thing people want to know when contemplating a new career is, "Are there specific educational requirements?" In truth, you don't need any formal education to become a capable event planner. If you have outstanding organizational skills, a keen eye for detail, exceptional communication skills, and a ton of experience in organizing events, then nothing can stop you from becoming an accomplished event planner.

Nevertheless, many event planners will later discover that the absence of a degree can limit their opportunities in booking more contract, since many clients, especially big companies, will only hire four-year degree graduates. Event planning requires a definite set of skills that can be learned through working towards a degree in communications, business, marketing, and public relations. These are just recommended degrees and are not mandatory for starting a career as an event planner. The preferred degree, however, is Hospitality Management. Many clients, especially in the U.S., purposefully choose to hire someone who boasts a Bachelor's Degree in Hospitality Management.

If you truly want to make a lifelong profession out of event planning, possibly starting your own business in the future, investing money and four years of your life to obtain a Hospitality Management degree, it can certainly be worth your while. The degree program includes a broad spectrum of knowledge that can be useful in event planning. You will have professional training and detailed instructions on communication, financial accounting, nutrition, food production, lodging operations, business, and economics.

Aside from enrolling in a bachelor's degree program in Hospitality and Management, you can also check out online certificate programs in this course. If you already have a Bachelor's degree in another field, you might consider online certificate programs in planning and management, communications, business, or other related programs. You should also check community education courses and see what useful courses you can take.

Other credentials that you can add to your resume as an event planner are certifications from professional organizations related to the event planning industry. The International Special Events Society (ISES) and the Meeting Professionals International (MPI) are among the organizations that provide certification in event planning. As long as you have gained a minimum of three years' experience in the industry and have taken and passed their written test, then it qualifies you for the title of Certified Special Events Professional (CSEP). You can also obtain a Certified Meeting Planners (CMP) certification.

Keep in mind that becoming a certified event planner can open more doors for you. Your chances of getting hired will increase as you gain certifications that help prove that you are capable of handling the tasks required of an event planner. Although not all clients will be looking for a degree or certifications, it can be a great advantage to have these in your resume anyway. If your goal is to open your own event planning business one day, having these credentials can be very beneficial for you.

Event planning may not require someone to have specific formal education and certifications but, in an industry where competition is fierce, an aspiring event planner must be willing to obtain some credentials.

Chapter 2: Training and Experience

As you probably already know, event planning involves a number of duties and responsibilities. Some of these include consulting with clients to discuss the event, checking the availability and price of possible venues and meeting with caterers, florists, vendors, and on-site staff. Many event planners also assist the guests, review expenses and doing accounting, but the most important duty of all is troubleshooting any snags that may arise before the event, and especially during the whole affair. The duties and responsibilities of an event planner can also vary depending on the type of event and the needs of the client.

Before becoming a full-fledged event planner, it helps to obtain a wide range of experience in the many aspects of event planning. Although you may have had a great deal of opportunities to organize family events, professional event planning can be much more challenging. Planning a dinner for twenty people certainly requires less work than organizing an event for fifty to two hundred guests. Having said that, it is best to familiarize yourself with all the facets of event planning. The best way to accomplish that is to get as much experience as you can in organizing all kinds of events.

If at this time you are looking to start a career as a special events planner, a very helpful stepping stone and an enriching experience is to work as an assistant for an established and a more experienced event planner. What better way to learn about the business than being under the tutelage of an expert in the field? By working as an assistant, you can learn about the various aspects of event planning. Assistants to event planners play an extremely important role in the organization of the whole event. They are exposed directly to the planning, operations, and management tasks of the event planner. Although, assistants are often assigned a myriad of chores which can be either related or unrelated to the event planning, working as an assistant is still the fastest and most effective way to learn about the industry. You can be assigned to booking venues, handling transportation, setting up meetings with vendors, talking to the caterers, etc. You will also meet people who may later become important contacts once you start your own career as an event planner, or when you open your own event planning business.

However, the biggest benefit that you may take away from an assistant position is not the exposure to the responsibilities of an event planner or meeting important contacts. When you work as an assistant, you are given a gamut of tasks that you must accomplish efficiently. But you really know that you are on your way to becoming more than just an assistant when you begin to also preemptively complete tasks that weren't assigned to you or anticipated. There is now a shift of perspective from assisting to planning, and this is how you will build the confidence that it takes to be a true event planner.

Working as an assistant to a reputable event planner can provide you with valuable experience and the necessary training you need to start a career or open a business in event planning. It's certainly the best way to learn the ropes. In future you can be confident in organizing your own events because you have obtained first-hand experience while working as an assistant.

Chapter 3: Networking

Perhaps one of the most essential tools of any capable event planner is the contact list, or rolodex. This is the roster of all the clients, vendors, caterers, suppliers, service providers, and others who can help make party planning a breeze. Usually, an event planner will keep a record of all the names, contact numbers, addresses, price lists, and other important information of people that he or she has worked with in the past. This will serve as a reference for any future contracts.

For individuals who are just starting in the event planning business, there's no need to fret. You will have numerous opportunities to meet a lot of people as you go through your career. The more events you coordinate, the more reliable contacts you'll be able to save in your book. However, you should also know that not all the people you meet along the way can be considered 'good' contacts. You'll meet crafty dealers and suppliers that will offer overpriced, substandard goods or services, and these must be distinguished from the ones that provide quality goods and services for the most reasonable rates. Gathering contacts for your event planning business later on can be a long journey. Nevertheless, it's an essential learning process for anyone aspiring to build a career in the event planning industry.

Again, if you have no idea where to start, a good way to meet florists, caterers, and vendors is to work as an assistant. Those that have interned for an event planning company have an advantage over those who have very little or no experience at all. Assistants to event planners often manage a lot of duties and they are exposed to almost all areas of event planning. This gives them the chance to meet countless individuals connected to the event planning industry. While working as an assistant, you can establish your contacts right away and make sure that you keep a good relationship with them for your future event planning aspirations.

However, those who have not had the chance to work as an assistant to event planners have other ways to establish contacts and build a network. Many successful event planners actually use the traditional, tried-and-tested method when it comes to establishing relations – approach people and talk to them. Traditional businessmen still place importance on meetings, presentations, and just being friendly. So, when you meet a prospective client, vendor, supplier, or anyone that you think can be of help to you later on in your event planning business, don't be afraid to approach them and start a conversation. Who knows? You might gain a reliable and a lifelong business contact.

Building a network of contacts makes your job as an event planner easier. If you need a caterer, a florist, or a venue, you can just look up someone from your extensive contact list. Having all these people in your phonebook and just a call away can make you a much more reliable and efficient event planner.

Chapter 4: Knowing Your Market

Once you become an event planner, you have to be thoroughly familiar with your market. The very first thing that you need to know about is the variety of clients you'll be working with and the occasions and celebrations that you will be planning. Basically, there are two potential markets for an event planning business. These are the corporate market and the social market.

The corporate market includes companies, nonprofit organizations, and charities. Many modern companies today host numerous company activities for their employees. These events include company outings, family picnics, and the more popular than ever team-building activities. There are also parties to celebrate the company's anniversary, awards and recognition nights, birthdays and holiday events. A large number of industries also hold quarterly, semi-annual, and annual conventions for reports on the company's progress. Companies in the U.S. spend tens of billions of dollars every year hosting millions of business meetings.

Events by nonprofit organizations can include civic events, tributes, memorials, fundraisers, awards ceremonies and recognition nights. During the elections, NGO's often host political rallies for candidates and their political parties. These events often require meticulous planning and will require the services of a skilled event planner. On the other hand, various charities host parties to attract more supporters. These charities often use these events to gather funding for their cause. Every year there are thousands of receptions, competitions, and galas held in the United States and all over the world.

The other kind of market for the event planning industry is the social market. Here event planners often work with families as main clients. Social events include family parties like Christening receptions, weddings, Sweet 16 parties, bat and bar mitzvah, birthday celebrations, weddings, and anniversaries. The social market is pretty stable and will continue to increase with more babies being born, people getting married, kids growing up, and people celebrating family events.

Most events for the corporate market will include hundreds to thousands of participants and will require specialized event planning skills. You may want to handle these kinds of events once you have had more experience in the industry. Now that you're just starting with your career, you can target smaller events in your locality and work your way up to organizing large-scale events later on. Meanwhile, there are countless events for the social market that can provide you a lot of valuable experience when it comes to event planning. One tip to remember in becoming an accomplished event planner is to treat all of your clients as important figures, and treat all your contracts as large-scale events. It means that you offer 100% effort and professionalism, whether the event is a kid's first birthday party or a political rally for a senator. One day, you might run your own event planning business and you'll be grateful for all the experience you gained from handling these small-scale events. Also, you may rely on your previous clients for references, referrals, and testimonials down the road, so you will certainly want to leave a great impression at every opportunity.

Now that you are aware of the possible target market in the business of event planning, you can build your goals around it. Would you be willing to work for both the corporate market and the social market, or will you focus on one? It is possible for you to choose the kinds of events you'd like to work on and the clients that you'd be willing to deal with. These are points to consider when you plan for your event planning career or when you open your own event planning business in the future.

Chapter 5: Advertising

Event planning is a very profitable profession. Naturally, the competition among event planners can be fierce. Those that have established their reputations have no trouble getting hired for jobs. However, for someone who is just beginning a career or starting a business in this industry, there are some things that can be done to improve the likelihood of getting hired to plan an event.

Like all professionals who wish to apply for work, the very first thing to build is your portfolio. A physical portfolio can be as simple as a clear book with all the pictures of the best events you've handled in the past. To create one, gather all the pictures that you have from an event that you have organized or helped to organize. Put together a sample of your best work for your future clients. Remember that you can start a portfolio even while you're working as an assistant to an event planner. Having a portfolio that you can bring with you and show to your clients anytime and anyplace can be very beneficial. At any event that you meet a potential client, you can just whip your book out from your bag and make an instant presentation. Another kind of portfolio is the online portfolio. Here you can post pictures of all your events on the internet and anybody can access it online. Having your own website can be a very smart decision, especially if you plan to open your own event planning company in the future. On your website you can include your resume, some information about you that you'd like your prospective clients to know, pictures from previous events, testimonials from prior clients, and your contact information. That way, people can easily call or email you if they're interested in your services.

Advertising your event planning services or business through popular social networking sites can also be very effective. Don't forget to link your website to your Facebook page, Twitter, and Instagram accounts. Social networks on the internet can be very powerful tools for marketing. At the same time, you can use your newsfeed to find potential clients. You also shouldn't take the traditional methods of advertising for granted. Newspaper ads, posters and media are still dependable ways to attract clients.

Once you have started working in the event planning industry, whether as an assistant, a full-fledged event planner, or a business owner; you must strive to build a good reputation with your clients, vendors, suppliers, and colleagues. Satisfied clients are your best advertisement. You won't need to spend anything and they will happily tell everyone how much they liked the way you organized their affair. Consequently, you need to establish good relations with everyone you deal with during your event planning. From the florists, caterers and vendors to colleagues, and workers, you must create a good business relationship with everyone. If you fail to do this, they won't want to work with you again in the future. That can be very bad for you if you're planning on opening your own event planning company in the future. People will talk about your event planning capabilities and spread information to one another through word of mouth, so be sure that what they will say about you is a positive advertisement. With a good reputation and effective advertising, you are on your way to becoming an in-demand event planner.

Conclusion

An event planning job can be very challenging, but it may be one of the top careers at this time. The demand for efficient, organized, and savvy event planners is constantly high and those associated with this industry will never worry about finding a market. In addition, event planning can be a very fulfilling profession. There is a great deal of satisfaction to be gained by providing a successful event, and it can also be a profitable career as well.

However, just like any other career or profession, event planning requires dedication and patience. Don't expect success to happen overnight. Invest your effort, time, and money in improving yourself. You can do so by continuously learning everything you can about this business. Don't stop at attaining a degree or certifications. Talk to and network with other event planners and assistants. They might have some insights or useful tips that they'd be able to share with you.

Hard work will always pay off, so gather as much knowledge and experience as you can in event planning and prepare yourself properly for a career in this profession. Nevertheless, don't be too hard on yourself. There are some things about the event planning business that you will learn naturally as you continue on with your journey.

Don't be afraid to try new things, and always seek advancement in this profession. If you are getting too comfortable in one area of event planning, tackle a challenge by mastering another aspect. Eventually you'll become an expert in all parts of event planning. From an assistant assigned to mostly menial tasks, ask to take on bigger roles such as management or coordination with a handful of vendors. From small-scale events, try handling larger-scale affairs. Soon enough, you'll be fully equipped to start your own company!

Last, I'd like to thank you for buying this book! If you enjoyed it or found it helpful, I'd greatly appreciate it if you'd take a moment to leave a review on Amazon. Thank you!